EVERYDAY SCIENCE

Turning Up The Heat:

Energy

Ann Fullick

Heinemann
LIBRARY

www.heinemann.co.uk/library

Visit our website to find out more information about **Heinemann Library** books.

To order:

 Phone 44 (0) 1865 888066

 Send a fax to 44 (0) 1865 314091

 Visit the Heinemann Bookshop at www.heinemann.co.uk/library to browse our catalogue and order online.

First published in Great Britain by Heinemann Library, Halley Court, Jordan Hill, Oxford OX2 8EJ, part of Harcourt Education Ltd. Heinemann is a registered trademark of Harcourt Education Ltd.

Editorial: Sarah Eason and Kathy Peltan
Design: Jo Hinton-Malivoire/Ascenders
Picture Research: Ruth Blair and Debra Weatherley
Production: Edward Moore

Originated by Ambassador Litho Ltd
Printed and bound in Hong Kong and China by South China Printing Co. Ltd.

The paper used to print this book comes from sustainable sources.

ISBN 0 431 16744 3
08 07 06 05 04
10 9 8 7 6 5 4 3 2 1

British Library Cataloguing in Publication Data
Fullick, Ann,
Turning up the Heat: Energy. – (Everyday science)
536
A full catalogue record for this book is available from the British Library.

Acknowledgements
The publishers would like to thank the following for permission to reproduce photographs: Action Plus p.**15**; Anthony Blake p.**25**; CORBIS/Ressmeyer pp.**40**, **48**; Fraser p.**12**; Getty pp.**4**, **9**, **13**, **16**, **24**, **37**; NASA p.**32**; Photodisc pp.**5**, **19**, **20**, **36**, **47**; Photodisc/Getty p.**31**; SPL pp.**10**, **49**; SPL/Science Industry & Business Library p.**34**; SPL/Frieder p.**42**; SPL/Hart-Davis p.**30**; SPL/Pasieka p.**38**; SPL/Sheila Terry p.**35**; SPL/Sher p.**23**; SPL/Syred p.**41**; SPL/TRL Ltd p.**14**; Steve Behr p.**6**; Still Pictures/Schytte p.**50**; Team Green/Shell p.**52**.

Cover photograph of runners crossing a finishing line reproduced by permission of Corbis.

Artwork by Ascenders apart from Jeff Edwards p.**29**; Mark Franklin pp.**17**, **33**.

The publishers would like to thank Robert Snedden for his assistance in the preparation of this book.

Every effort has been made to contact copyright holders of any material reproduced in this book. Any omissions will be rectified in subsequent printings if notice is given to the publishers.

Contents

Words appearing in bold, **like this**, are explained in the Glossary.

Energy everywhere

Wherever you are, whatever you are doing, **energy** is sure to be involved. You use lighting when it gets dark, heating when it gets cold, hot water for washing, a cooker and probably a car. You listen to the radio and the CD player, sometimes you watch television; you move about the house and you eat food. All of these things involve energy.

What is energy?

We often talk about energy: 'You have a lot of energy today', 'Sugary foods give you lots of energy', 'A low-energy appliance', 'Save energy'. Saying the word is one thing, but saying exactly what we mean by it is a different matter. It can be roughly defined as 'what is needed for any activity to take place'.

Plenty going on
Look hard at this picture and see how many different uses of energy you can spot.

Energy varieties

The Universe is full of energy. Much of it is what we call low-grade energy – it is there but is not of use because it is so spread out. The energy we can use every day is concentrated energy. This comes in different forms. Electrical energy, light energy, sound energy and heat energy are just a few familiar ones. **Kinetic energy**, **potential energy** and chemical energy are also essential parts of our everyday lives.

Fierce but friendly
We transfer the stored chemical energy in logs into heat energy to warm us.

One exciting fact about energy is that it cannot be created or destroyed – it is simply transferred from one form into another. When you flick a light switch, the electrical energy travelling through the wires is transferred into the light energy you see in the light bulb and the heat energy you feel coming off it. In the same way, the chemical energy in the food you eat is transferred into heat energy, kinetic energy and more chemical energy in the chemicals making up the cells of your body. Most energy ends up as part of the spread-out, low-grade energy filling the Universe.

Using energy carefully

Energy is everywhere we look, from the spectacular lightning bolt to the slow all-day, everyday release of energy in our bodies that keeps us alive. Energy works for us all the time, but its misuse causes real problems. The explosive chemicals used in bombs and missiles, the fires that can destroy vast areas of countryside and the global climate changes that result, partly at least, from our use of **fossil fuels** are all part of the energy picture. We must use our energy resources carefully and responsibly to get the most out of them, while doing as little harm as possible to the world around us.

Measuring energy

Because **energy** comes in so many different forms, we use different types of instrument to measure it and its effects. Can you remember the last time you were really poorly? Someone probably felt your forehead to see if you were abnormally hot, a sure sign that your body is fighting an infection. A transfer of heat energy increases the **temperature** of an object, whether it's a kettle full of water or your body. Your skin is very sensitive to changes in temperature, but touching something gives only a rough indication of how hot it is. To measure accurately something's temperature, or a change in temperature, we use an instrument called a **thermometer**.

How does a thermometer work?

The mercury bulb thermometer works on the principle that as liquids get hotter their volume increases (they expand), and when they cool their volume decreases (they contract).

Hot or cold?
The temperatures of household items vary enormously. It is sometimes useful to be able to measure them.

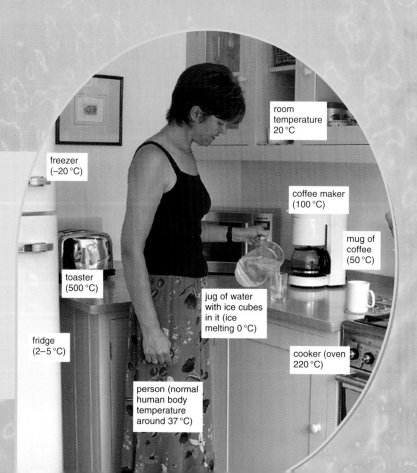

room temperature 20 °C

freezer (−20 °C)

coffee maker (100 °C)

mug of coffee (50 °C)

toaster (500 °C)

jug of water with ice cubes in it (ice melting 0 °C)

fridge (2–5 °C)

cooker (oven 220 °C)

person (normal human body temperature around 37 °C)

A mercury thermometer has a bulb containing liquid mercury with a very narrow tube leading out of it. When the bulb is placed in a warm liquid the mercury heats up, expanding up the tube. The hotter the substance, the more the mercury expands and the further its level in the tube rises. The thermometer has been **calibrated** so that certain levels of mercury represent particular temperatures. The same principle is used in thermometers that measure outdoor or indoor temperatures, although here alcohol is used instead of mercury.

Temperature scales

The Celsius and the Fahrenheit scales are temperature scales. Their inventors made certain numbers represent certain key temperatures and worked from there. For instance, Celsius called the boiling and freezing points of water 100° and 0° respectively. In the Fahrenheit scale, they are 212° and 32°. In the Absolute (Kelvin) scale, water boils at 373 K and freezes at 273 K.

More ways of measuring temperature

In our homes are many places where we need to control the temperature, such as in ovens, fridges, freezers and heating systems. For example, for cooking we need to put energy into the oven until it reaches a certain temperature, and when the food has cooked we need to switch off the energy until the temperature falls, or the food will burn. This system involves a **thermostat**. At the heart of a thermostat there is often a bimetallic strip – two metals joined together. One expands more when it heats than the other, and this makes the strip bend. In an oven the strip bends so that at a given temperature an electrical circuit is broken. This either directly cuts off the electricity heating the oven or reduces the flow of gas into the oven by narrowing the opening of a valve in the gas supply. Then, as the strip cools down and straightens, the contact is renewed and the oven heats up again. In fridges the opposite happens – the strip completes an electrical circuit as the temperature rises, then electrical energy is used to cool the contents of the fridge again.

Temperature-sensitive materials that change colour at different temperatures can also be useful. They can be quite accurate, like the fever strips used to check the temperature of very young children, or just fun, like the mood rings people wear.

More energy measuring

Food contains the **energy** we depend on for life. Look on any food packaging and you will see lists of ingredients. These usually include the energy content of the food, often shown in both **calories** and joules.

Measuring food's energy

The amount of energy contained in a food can be found using a process known as **calorimetry**. An accurately weighed amount of the food is burned in pure oxygen. The heat given off is used to heat a known volume of water in a device called a **calorimeter**. The **temperature** of the water before and after heating is measured, and the change in temperature can be used to work out how much heat energy was produced by burning the food. Next time you look at the energy content of your food, just imagine all the burning and measuring that has taken place to give you that information!

Measuring electricity

Electrical energy is needed for almost all the machines and gadgets we use. The television, washing machine, dishwasher and computer all need electricity. Shops, offices, hospitals and factories rely on a constant supply of electrical energy. When we measure electrical energy, several things have to be taken into account. Most importantly, the amount of electrical energy that an appliance transfers into heat, light or whatever else is required will depend on two factors. These are how long the appliance is switched on for, and how much electrical energy it can transfer in a given time (its **power**). Power is measured in **watts** (W) or **kilowatts** (kW). 1 kilowatt is equivalent to 1000 watts. Power for small appliances like hair-driers is measured in watts, but many bigger appliances transfer energy at a rate best measured in kilowatts. The amount of electricity we use in our homes is measured using a meter.

Energy units

The basic energy unit is the joule, named after 19th-century British scientist James Prescott Joule. Energy units were formerly called calories, and food energy values are often given in calories and joules – scientists use joules but most people still use calories. 4.2 joules of heat energy raise the temperature of 1 g of water by 1° C. (4.2 joules = 1 calorie.) Confusingly, 'food calories' are really kilocalories (C) – each worth a thousand calories.

Lighting-up time
*Light meters are used in switches for street lights.
When the light level drops below a certain point,
the light is automatically switched on.*

Measuring light energy

Light energy is a constant part of our lives. It enables us to see,
and provides energy for all the plants in the world to make their
food. There are various ways of measuring light energy. They often
involve a light meter. A light meter samples the light intensity over
a given area and works out the average light intensity there. Light
meters built in to cameras make sure exactly the right amount of
light reaches the film to take the best possible picture. Light
meters also play an important part in some sports. In cricket, the
umpires use light meters to decide if there is sufficient light for
play to continue safely, and if not the game is stopped.

Living sensors

Energy is vital to our existence, and our bodies are well-tuned energy-sensing machines. We see because our eyes are sensitive to light energy. They respond to changes in light intensity by altering the amount of light that they let in to the delicate light-sensitive cells at the back of the eyeball.

Light-sensitive eyes

You can see this working for yourself. Look closely at the pupils of your eyes in a well lit mirror – they will look fairly small because the light intensity is high and so your eyes respond by limiting the amount of light getting in. Now cover your eyes with your hands for a minute or so. Keep your eyes open. You are providing yourself with a very low light intensity. Move your hands away quickly and watch carefully what happens to your pupils – they should be much wider open after being in the dark, to let more light in, but then shrink down again as you expose your eyes to bright light again.

Plants and light

Plants use light energy from the Sun to make sugar from carbon dioxide and water in a process called **photosynthesis**. They change the direction of their leaves throughout the day to get as much light as possible. Plants growing in shade will grow upwards extra fast, hurrying to capture more light energy from the Sun. If they cannot reach sunlight, many plants grow bigger leaves to catch more light energy.

Sound-sensitive ears

You are sensitive to sound energy too – your ears detect sounds over quite a wide range, but cannot hear sounds at the extremes of the range. Other animals are far more sensitive to sound energy than we are. Dogs can hear whistles that we cannot, because they are sensitive to high-pitched sounds that our ears cannot pick up. The bats that you might see fluttering around on summer evenings use sound energy to fly in dim light, and to detect their insect prey.

Guardian cells
Your skin contains nerve cells, shown here in orange, that detect and measure heat energy. The nerve cells carry information around our bodies.

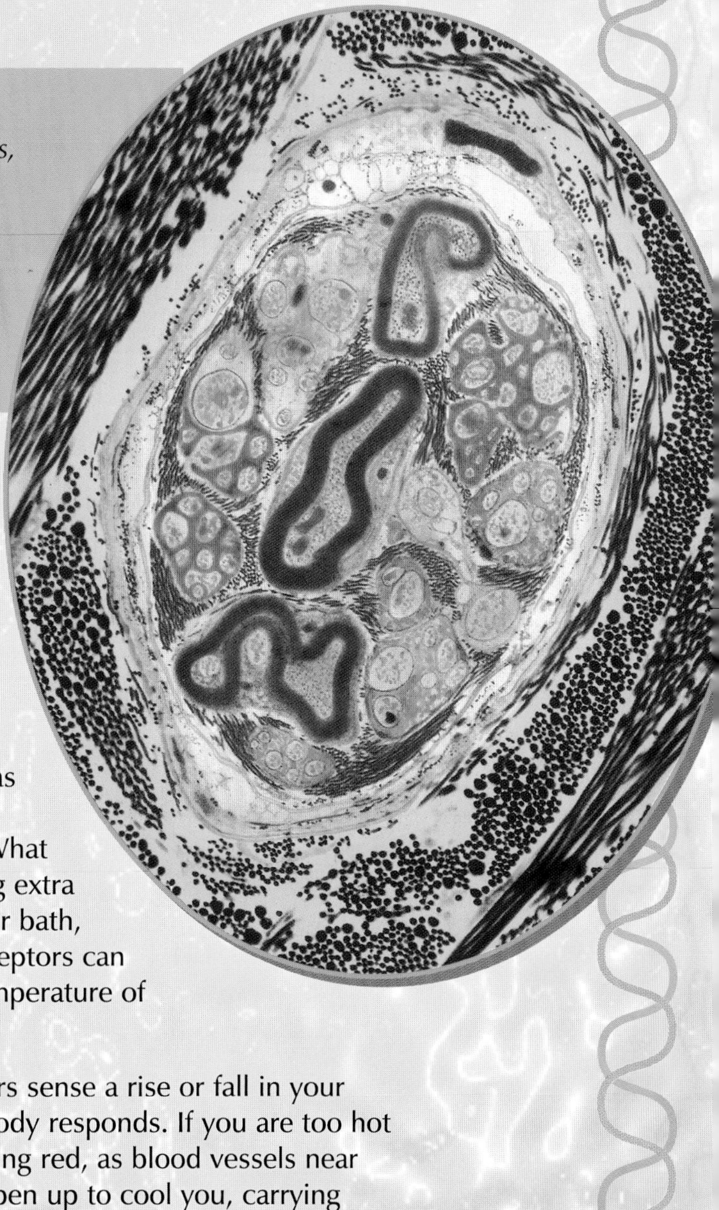

Heat-sensitive skin

The human skin is very sensitive to temperature differences. Although we use **thermometers** when people are ill, parents can usually tell if their child has a temperature simply by touching their forehead. What is more, if you are running extra hot or cold water into your bath, your skin temperature receptors can pick up a rise or fall in temperature of only 0.5°C.

If your temperature sensors sense a rise or fall in your body temperature, your body responds. If you are too hot you start sweating and going red, as blood vessels near the surface of your skin open up to cool you, carrying more blood to the surface of the skin where you will lose heat energy. If you are too cold your blood supply is shunted away from the skin to the vital organs and you start shivering to generate heat. You also get goose pimples as your body tries to fluff up your hair to trap an insulating layer of air and hold on to as much heat energy as possible.

Complications

Measuring energy is harder than it might seem. Next time you are sipping a hot chocolate, think about all the energy that has been used to warm it up. One way of measuring this is to take the temperature of the drink – if it is at 50 °C you know it contains more energy than if it was only at 40 °C. There is more to it than this, though. What size is your mug? It takes more energy to heat a big mug of chocolate up to 50 °C than a small mug.

How much energy?

Now think about a swimming pool. The water in a pool is normally about 30 °C, which is not hot. But there is a huge quantity of water in a swimming pool, so an enormous amount of energy is needed to heat it up. It is important to remember that the amount of heat energy in an object cannot be measured simply by measuring its temperature.

Working hard
Heating the water in a swimming pool to only 30 °C uses much more energy than heating a kettle of water to 100 °C.

Doing work

One of the important facts about energy is that it is used for doing **work**. That work might be heating things up, or moving things about. When you visit a department store, the things you want to buy always seem to be on one of the higher floors – maybe 15 metres up. You have two choices about how to get there. You might run up the stairs, or you might use the lift. Moving your body **mass** against the force of gravity for a distance of 15 metres takes considerable energy. This can be measured by multiplying your weight in **newtons** by the distance it is lifted in metres. The lift will have done exactly the same amount of work to lift you as your legs, because it will have lifted your mass up 15 metres. (For the sake of this explanation we ignore the weight of the lift and the work that has to be done to lift it up.) The amount of energy used will be the same, but there is one big difference: the lift will probably have moved you upwards faster than your legs.

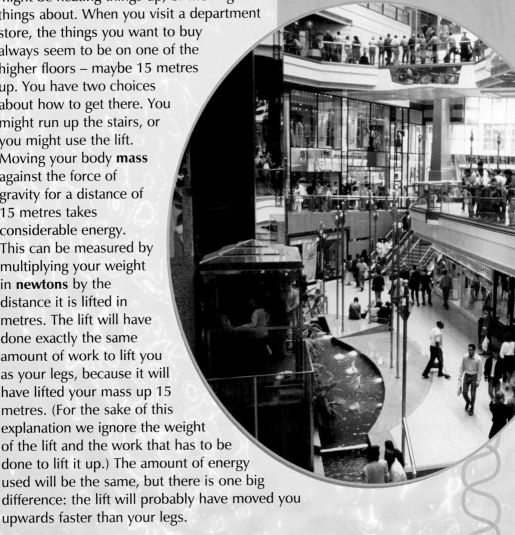

Taking the strain
Moving upwards feels easier in a lift, because our legs are not having to provide the power to lift our body weight.

Another important measurement when considering energy is power, the rate at which energy is transferred from one place to another, or at which work is done. Although the lift and your legs will have done the same amount of work in moving you up, the lift motor has used more power than your leg muscles if it has lifted you up in a shorter time.

Kinetic energy

All forms of **energy** can be divided into two basic types. Energy involving movement is **kinetic energy**, while energy that is stored is **potential energy**. Kinetic energy involves any kind of movement. It can be you running, or the movements of molecules, atoms and **electrons** that are too minute for us to see but that affect us all the time.

Energy in motion

The simplest form of kinetic energy to understand is the energy of large moving objects. As you move around, you have kinetic energy; you feel its impact if someone runs into you. The amount of energy a moving object has depends on its **mass** and its speed. A heavy person running at the same speed as a light person will have more kinetic energy. A light person running really fast may have as much kinetic energy as, or more than, a heavy person moving slowly.

Kinetic energy explains why it is so important for cars to travel slowly in built-up areas. Because kinetic energy increases at the same rate as the square of the speed, a speed increase of just a few miles an hour increases the kinetic energy of the vehicle enormously. This means the car is more likely to cause severe injuries or death if it hits anyone. Lowering your speed quickly reduces the kinetic energy of the car.

Deadly speed
A speed reduction of only 10 miles an hour can mean that a person is only badly shaken rather than killed.

Moving things together

Rub your hands together briskly – what do you notice? They should feel warmer. When any two things move against each other they get hotter as a result of **friction**. If you feel car tyres after a journey they may feel hot. We use oil in vehicle engines to prevent the working parts from rubbing directly against each other and getting so hot that they expand and stick together. We heat our homes and our bath water, we cook. All of these things involve heat energy – but what are we really talking about?

To understand heat energy we have to understand **matter**. Everything is made up of tiny particles (atoms and molecules) that we cannot see. These particles are all moving; this movement produces heat energy, so heat energy is kinetic energy. When an object is hot, its atoms and molecules are 'excited' – they contain high energy and are moving rapidly.

Imagine some balloons hung outside. If the day is hot the balloons get bigger and might burst, but if they are left out all night they get cold and become smaller and shrunken. Why? When particles have high levels of energy and are moving around rapidly, they take up more space. This is why things expand (grow bigger) when they are hot. When the atoms and molecules slow down as they cool, they take up less space, so things grow smaller (contract) as they cool down.

Kinetic energy as heat

Imagine a bar of chocolate that has been left inside a hot car for a few hours. The gooey, melted result shows us clearly that heat **energy** can travel. Cats know this; if there is a particularly warm spot in a house, a pet cat will certainly find it and enjoy the transfer of heat energy from the warm spot to itself.

Conduction

Have you ever left a metal spoon in a saucepan on the hob, and then gone back to stir the food? Do not try it – the spoon will be painfully hot! Heat energy flows from an area of high **temperature** to one with a lower temperature. In solids this is called **conduction**, occurring when energy is transferred from one atom or molecule to another touching it. Conduction is partly to blame for the fact that your mug of coffee cools down – the heat energy does not disappear, it is transferred into the mug and the air. Heat energy travels more easily through some materials – such as metals – that are known as good conductors of heat than it does through others, such as glass, which are poor conductors.

Very hot
Heat energy travels, which is why sitting around a campfire to get warm works so well.

Thermos flasks

To keep things hot we have to prevent heat loss by conduction, convection and radiation. The **vacuum** flask is designed to minimize the transfer of heat energy in or out. Factors that work to prevent heat loss also prevent heat gain, so flasks are just as good at keeping things cold as keeping things hot – ideal for ice cream as well as coffee on picnics!

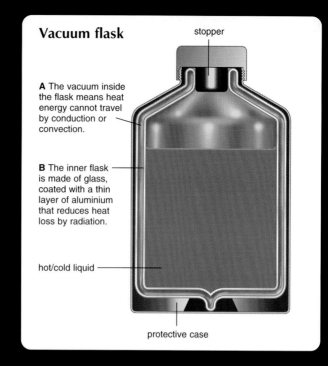

Vacuum flask

stopper

A The vacuum inside the flask means heat energy cannot travel by conduction or convection.

B The inner flask is made of glass, coated with a thin layer of aluminium that reduces heat loss by radiation.

hot/cold liquid

protective case

Convection

The principle of heat energy being transferred from a hotter to a colder area also applies in liquids and gases (**fluids**). This usually happens when movement – known as a **convection** current – occurs in the fluid. As the fluid grows warmer near a source of heat it expands, becoming less dense, and so rises through the cooler (denser) fluid. It is replaced by cooler fluid, which is heated in its turn. Convection currents affect everyday actions such as putting ice cubes in a drink (the cooled liquid sinks and is replaced by slightly warmer liquid, which in turn comes into contact with the cold ice and sinks), or running extra hot water in the bath.

Radiation

Everything emits electromagnetic radiation on many different wavelengths, some of which we can see as visible light. The hotter an object is, the more short-wavelength infrared radiation it gives off. So when something is really hot, it glows red. A fire glows red as it provides us with heat. We can use this heat to grill food.

Kinetic energy as electricity

Most of us never think about electrical **energy**. We flick the switches or grab the remote without ever wondering what it really is, this electricity we rely on. Electrical energy is one of the most useful forms of energy because it can easily be transferred into other types of energy, such as heat, light or movement. Read more about this on pages 34 and 35.

Inside atoms

Just like heat energy, electrical energy is actually a form of **kinetic energy**. In this case, it is not whole atoms and molecules that are moving, but **electrons**. No one can actually see atoms, so what we know about their structure is a scientific model. That is, a picture based on all the different evidence we have, which attempts to explain the way atoms behave. The current model of an atom has a positively charged central nucleus containing particles called **neutrons** (heavy neutral particles) and **protons** (heavy positively charged particles) held together by very strong forces. Moving incredibly quickly around the nucleus is a cloud of negatively charged electrons (very light particles with a **negative charge**). The atom is electrically neutral because the number of protons and electrons is always exactly equal, and in most cases very stable.

Supplying the need

Huge quantities of electricity can be moved from place to place quite simply in metal wires. The wires on the huge overhead pylons of the National Grid can carry very much more electrical energy than the wires in your home – up to 400,000 volts compared with 220 volts in your home. **Transformers** are used to ensure that the electricity arriving at your plug sockets is exactly the right **voltage** to allow your appliances to work safely.

In most atoms the electrons circle the nucleus, held close by the protons' **positive charges**. Sometimes, however – for instance in metals – the electrons are freed from this structure, so they can move around. It is this movement of electrons, or flow of charge, that we call electricity.

To give you an idea of how many electrons are involved in the electricity we use every day, it takes an estimated 6.28 billion billion electrons to keep a small torch lit for just one second!

High wires

Electricity pylons carry vast amounts of electrical energy and distribute it all over the country.

Conductors and insulators

Materials through which electricity can flow are known as **conductors**. The human body is quite a good conductor of electricity, which is why we have to be so careful when we deal with it. Our heartbeat and many other functions of the body are controlled by electrical impulses, so if a big electric shock passes through our body it is likely to interfere with these vital functions – electric shocks can kill!

Fortunately many other materials, such as wood, rubber and plastic, do not have charged particles that can move, and so cannot conduct electricity. These materials are known as **insulators** and we use them to protect us from electric shocks. This is why electric wires are made of copper in the middle – to conduct the electricity – with plastic coatings on the outside to insulate us from the current inside.

Electricity in the wild

The electricity we use is 'domesticated' electricity. We make it, we send it through the system and use it when we want it. However, electricity turns up in other places in our lives – where we cannot always control it with a switch!

Static electricity

Have you ever had a tiny electric shock stepping on to an escalator or out of a car? Have you ever rubbed a balloon on your jumper and stuck it on the wall? If so, you have experienced **static electricity**. The electricity we have looked at so far involves a flow of charge, but static electricity is rather different. It is a build-up of charge in one place – that is, it is static (still). Electrons are rubbed off one material and build up on another. The amount of charge increases, until the difference between the negative and positive charges on the two materials (the **potential difference**) becomes so big that the electrons flow back to where they came from. This produces a small spark and an electric shock for anyone who happens to be in the way.

Thunder and lightning
Electrical storms are awe-inspiring and involve enormous amounts of electrical energy.

Static electricity around us

Static electricity builds up around us in everyday activities. Stroking a pet or combing your hair can cause enough static electricity to build up to have visible effects. Your hair may stand on end as the charged strands repel one another, or the cat might run off as a spark jumps!

Benjamin Franklin

In June 1752, US scientist Benjamin Franklin carried out an incredibly dangerous experiment. He flew a kite into a thundercloud to prove that lightning is electricity. He tied a key to the end of the kite's string, and saw and felt a spark jump from the key to his finger, showing that electricity was involved. He was incredibly lucky – if lightning had struck the kite, Franklin would almost certainly have been killed!

Using static electricity

Static electricity can be useful. Photocopiers and laser printers use a light-sensitive drum that develops different areas of static charge depending on the amount of light falling on it. Particles of toner are attracted to the static charge, then transferred to the paper to produce an image.

However, static electricity can also cause problems. Static sparks can cause explosions in fuel tanks, so great care has to be taken when delivering fuel to filling stations and refuelling aircraft.

Lightning strikes

Some people are terrified of thunderstorms. Others find them exhilarating and enjoy watching one of nature's most dramatic displays. Whatever your view, thunderstorms are probably the most spectacular example of static electricity we can see.

In storm clouds, ice particles and water drops caught in swirling air currents tumble against each other, losing and gaining electrons and becoming charged with static electricity. The top of the cloud becomes positively charged and the bottom negatively charged. If the charges in the cloud build up enough, they force a path to the ground through the air and discharge as a lightning flash. The electrical energy is transferred into light, heat and sound.

The **temperature** of a lightning strike is 20–30,000 °C – more than three times as hot as the surface of the Sun! The surrounding air heats up and expands so quickly that it travels faster than the speed of sound, breaking the sound barrier and causing **sonic booms** – thunder!

How fast does sound travel?

A lightning bolt and thunder clap begin at the same time. Sound travels at about 340 metres per second. Light is almost a million times faster! Count the seconds between flash and boom, and divide by three – the storm was that many kilometres away.

Kinetic energy as sound

Sit very quietly and listen hard. What can you hear? Voices, a clock ticking, music, traffic – whatever you hear, you are detecting sound. We live in a world full of sound, all caused when objects vibrate.

Sound measure

English clergyman William Derham measured the speed of sound fairly accurately in 1708. He stood on top of a church, watched a cannon being fired 19 kilometres away, and measured the time that passed before he heard the 'boom'.

Sound waves

When a guitar string is plucked, the vibrations push rapidly backwards and forwards on the air around it, making the air particles collide. As they collide, **energy** is passed from one to another as a travelling pressure wave. Because sound is made up of travelling pressure waves, it has to travel through a medium, such as air, water or metal. Sound cannot travel through a **vacuum**.

We can feel sound vibrations as they are made. Press gently on your voice box – the lumpy bit in your throat – as you speak. You can feel the vibrations it produces.

When you strike a drum, the skin is pushed in as you hit it, then moves out again. It **flexes** backwards and forwards very quickly, pushing on the air molecules around it and making the air pressure fall and then rise. These pressure changes are then passed on through the air.

This movement is a form of **kinetic energy** and we call it sound. Sound waves are measured in Hertz (Hz). 1 Hertz equals one vibration per second. The normal range of hearing for a young person is 20–20,000 Hz.

Did you know?

Fishermen in trawlers use sound waves to find shoals of fish. The sound bounces back off the fish, and the trawlermen cast their nets.

A sound's loudness depends on the amount of energy carried in the sound waves. Big vibrations have big energy and produce loud sounds – **sonic booms**. The shock waves from explosions can cause us physical damage, from burst eardrums to damaged internal organs.

Sound speeds

Sound passes through solids and liquids faster than through air because they are denser, and so the vibrations move faster from one particle to another.

Material	Speed of sound travelling through
air	343 metres per sec (at 20 °C and sea level)
water	1500 metres per sec
steel	6000 metres per sec

Using sound energy

We use sound all the time to communicate. We have developed many ways of communicating over greater and greater distances, by converting sound energy into electrical signals that travel thousands of miles before being converted back into sound energy again. But we use sound in other ways as well. If you shout loudly in a tunnel the sound waves you have created will hit the walls around you and bounce back, forming an echo. Scientists use echoes from sound at frequencies above 20,000 Hz. This is known as **ultrasound**. Doctors use it to see inside our bodies.

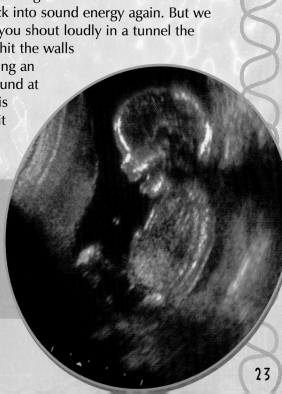

Bouncing echoes
Ultrasound allows us to see developing babies before they are born. A scanner displays the 'echoes' as an image on a screen.

Light **energy** illuminates our lives. Light energy from the Sun not only enables us to see, it enables us to exist. Plants use light energy – around 10^{19} **kilojoules** per year – to convert carbon dioxide and water into sugar and oxygen. In this process they provide us with the food we need to eat and the oxygen we need to breathe! So light energy is of vital importance to our everyday life on Earth.

What is light?

Light is a form of energy that travels in waves. Light waves can travel through a **vacuum**, which is why light from objects millions of miles away in space can reach the Earth. Another important property of light becomes obvious when you use a torch. If you are moving around in the dark, depending on the light from a torch, you cannot use your torch beam to see round corners. This is because light rays always travel in straight lines. They can be **reflected** (they change direction as they bounce off a solid object) or **refracted** (they change direction as they pass through different materials and so change speed).

We know **kinetic energy** involves movement. So how fast does light travel? The most accurate measurements put the speed of light at 299,792,458 metres per second (or around 300,000 kilometres per second). That really is impressive – nothing in the entire known Universe travels faster!

Big lamp
The amount of light energy produced by the Sun is vast – around 10^{31} (100,000,000,000,000,000,000,000,000,000,000) kilojoules every year! It provides the energy for all food production on Earth.

Different wavelengths, different speeds

The light that we see is known as white light or visible light. It is actually made up of different coloured light rays combined together. White light can be split up into its different colours by passing it through a special piece of glass, a 'prism', which separates all the different colours into a spectrum. Each colour of light has a different wavelength – red light has the longest wavelength and violet light the shortest – and they travel at different speeds. So each colour is refracted by a different amount and they bend at different angles. Red bends the least and violet the most. The wavelength order of the colours is red, orange, yellow, green, blue, indigo and violet. In a rainbow, each tiny droplet of water acts as a prism, splitting the sunlight into the spectrum that we see arcing across the sky.

More than colours

The different colours of light that we can see belong to a much larger family of waves, most of which we cannot see – the electromagnetic spectrum. As well as visible light it includes radio waves, microwaves, infrared light, ultraviolet light, **X-rays** and **gamma rays**. So the electromagnetic spectrum touches almost everything in our lives, from domestic appliances in the home to life-saving medical treatments.

Easy peas
Microwave ovens make heating food quick and easy, using kinetic energy.

Microwave ovens

For many of us the microwave has become essential, because it heats food up so fast. The way it works illustrates the link between the movement of atoms and molecules and heat energy. A microwave oven produces electromagnetic waves, called microwaves, which are absorbed by water, fat and sugar molecules in the food. As they absorb the microwaves, the molecules become excited and move around rapidly. The food gets hot!

Potential energy

Most forms of **kinetic energy** are obvious – you can hear sounds, see things moving and feel the impact if they collide with you. Other types of **energy** are less obvious. Most of this hidden energy is what we call **potential energy**. It is stored energy, available for use when we need it.

Energy up high

Lift a ball over your head. You had to use energy for this, and this energy was transferred to the ball. While it is up in the air it contains gravitational potential energy, so called because the energy has been given to it by moving it against gravity, and once you let go of it, that potential energy is transferred into movement or kinetic energy as the ball falls to the ground. Anything lifted above the surface of the Earth has gravitational potential energy and will, given the opportunity, transfer that energy into kinetic energy by falling back down to Earth.

Power and beauty
One of the most dramatic of all natural examples of gravitational potential energy must be a waterfall.

Picture yourself riding your bicycle up a hill. When you get to the top of the hill you have gravitational potential energy. That energy can be transferred into movement as you freewheel all the way down again! You can enjoy the ride without having to do any work.

Potential energy in nature

There are some spectacular examples of gravitational potential energy in nature. Imagine walking out in the countryside and finding a waterfall. Stand at the top, near the relatively calm water – listen to the roar of the fall, the movement of the water and the rainbows dancing in the spray as tonnes of water transfer gravitational potential energy in the pool at the top into kinetic and sound energy as the water falls to the rocks beneath.

Elastic energy and springy springs

Have you ever used a trampoline, or just bounced about on your bed? These activities depend on another sort of potential energy – **elastic potential energy**. This is the energy stored in something because of a change in its shape. When a spring or an elastic band is stretched, energy is stored in the material. When the stretch is released, the stored energy is transferred and is usually used to produce movement – bouncing you up into the air from the trampoline, for example!

Elastic energy is very important in clockwork mechanisms, where a key is used to wind up a metal spring and the energy stored in the spring is then transferred slowly into the movement of the hands of a clock or the parts of a toy. At one time all clocks ran on clockwork. Today many clocks still need regular winding, but many others rely instead on the chemical potential energy of batteries. We also use the elastic potential energy of springs – in our mattresses and in the suspension in our cars.

Using elastic energy

A great example of the use of elastic energy is the pole vault. Watch a pole vaulter run and plant the pole, bending it right down before taking off. The elastic potential energy stored in the bent pole is used to lift the vaulter 5 or 6 metres up. At the top of the vault, the pole is dropped; the vaulter has plenty of gravitational potential energy, quickly transferred back into movement energy in the fall back to the ground.

Chemical potential energy

Most of us have used battery-operated toys and gadgets – for example, personal stereos, games consoles and torches. But a Game Boy does not work in its packaging, and an empty torch is no help to see in the dark. Put batteries in and as if by magic the graphics appear on the screen and a beam of light shines out from the torch. But it is not magic that starts things working – the changes are brought about as the stored **chemical potential energy** in the batteries is transferred into useful electrical, light and sound **energy**.

What is chemical potential energy?

To understand what chemical potential energy is we have to look once more into the sub-microscopic world of atoms, molecules and **electrons**.

An atom is made up of a nucleus surrounded by electrons. Atoms join together to form molecules by making **chemical bonds**. Energy is involved in making and breaking these bonds. The important thing about chemical bonds is that energy is needed to break them, and energy is released when new bonds are formed.

Did you know?

In 1938 an archaeologist digging near Baghdad, Iraq found some little jars with asphalt stoppers, containing iron rods surrounded by copper cylinders. Scientists think these may have been batteries, possibly used to apply gold coatings to silver jewellery. They are 2000 years old.

Batteries contain chemicals that act as an energy store. Energy is released when new bonds are formed in the chemical reactions that take place inside the battery. The energy released as these chemical reactions take place is transferred into electrical energy, which can then be employed to do useful things like operate games and torches.

The right battery for the job

The amount of chemical potential energy in a battery depends on several things. One is the chemical combination in the battery. Silver-zinc batteries can provide more energy than alkaline batteries of the same size, but cost a lot more, so our everyday batteries are alkaline.

Inventing batteries

The first battery was invented in 1799 by Italian scientist Alessandro Volta. He used a pile of copper and zinc discs separated by cardboard discs soaked in salt water, with a wire coming out of the top and the bottom. The problem with using this pile was that the wet cardboard kept drying up! The type of battery we use was invented in 1865 by a Frenchman, Georges Leclanché.

Another factor is the size of the battery. Compare the size of the battery in your car to the size of battery in a personal stereo or your watch! Obviously the car battery contains far more chemical potential energy – but have you ever tried lifting one? The type of battery you use depends on both the amount of energy you need and the situation you need it in. Tiny batteries are used for things like watches and heart pacemakers, while enormous batteries are needed for juggernauts and tanks.

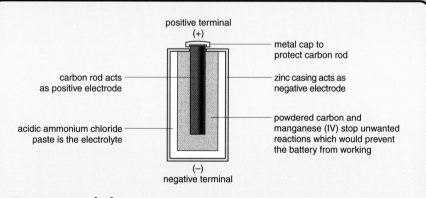

positive terminal (+)

metal cap to protect carbon rod

carbon rod acts as positive electrode

zinc casing acts as negative electrode

acidic ammonium chloride paste is the electrolyte

powdered carbon and manganese (IV) stop unwanted reactions which would prevent the battery from working

(–) negative terminal

Battery revealed
*The inside of one type of battery – the chemicals inside the battery are **corrosive** and so are contained within the outer case.*

Pops, crackles and big bangs

Matches are an amazing invention. We take them for granted, yet the little blob on the top of each match saves so much time and effort. Striking a match involves **friction**. Movement energy is transferred into heat energy, and that heat triggers a reaction in the chemicals on the head of the match – we have a useful, controlled flame. Chemical potential energy is used to produce heat and light.

Making it easy
Matches give us a form of chemical potential energy so we can have fire wherever and whenever we want.

Explosions

Celebrations often include crackers and party poppers. The bang when you pull the string on your party popper and the energy that shoots the streamers up into the air also come from the chemical potential energy stored in the chemicals inside the popper. On a bigger scale, the explosions we see on our TV screens caused by missiles or, more peaceably, in firework displays, are also caused by chemical potential energy. The explosive chemicals are relatively safe to handle. They can be positioned in a warhead on a missile, or in the fireworks before a display, and do not explode. Once a small amount of heat or electrical energy is added to them, however, there is a massive chemical reaction that gives out huge quantities of energy. Enormous amounts of chemical potential energy are converted into light, heat, sound and movement in the form of an explosion.

The potential in petrol

One form of chemical potential energy that most of us use every day is the potential energy in fuels. When petrol or diesel is burnt in air, as in a car engine, the potential energy is released and transferred into movement energy, heat and sound. This chemical potential energy is used to move millions of vehicles about on our roads every day.

Food for thought

Most of what we do with our bodies needs energy, and that energy is supplied by the chemical potential energy present in the chemical bonds of our food. The main types of food molecule that we eat are proteins, carbohydrates and fats. These three contain different numbers and types of chemical bond. As our bodies break down our food, we release the potential chemical energy and convert it into other forms of chemical energy that are easily used by our cells.

Some of the chemicals we eat – such as the **cellulose** in plant material – we cannot digest, and so cannot release their chemical potential energy. Other substances, particularly carbohydrates, are easily broken down to release useable energy. So different foods contain different amounts of available energy, which is why some are more fattening than others. If we eat too much food with plenty of available energy, we will take in more energy than we need. Our body will use the excess to store potential energy in the form of fat.

Dish up
We do not usually think of a plate of food as chemical potential energy, but that's exactly what it is.

Nuclear energy

Many forms of **energy**, such as light, heat and sound, are obvious in our everyday lives. One form of energy, though, is present everywhere, yet we are largely unaware of it. That is the energy present in every atom.

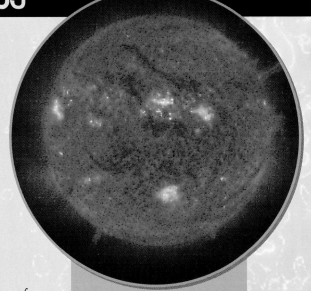

Our life-giver
The Sun lights and warms our world. It is the source of energy for most life on our planet.

Inside atoms

The forces inside the nucleus of an atom are immensely powerful, and the energy released when they are broken is enormous. **Nuclear reactions** and nuclear energy are familiar terms to most of us, but we do not always recognize just how much we rely on them.

The nuclear Sun

The Sun, which is the main energy source for Earth, is basically a massive nuclear reactor. It is a vast ball of gas – mainly hydrogen with some helium – and nuclear reactions are continually taking place within it, releasing the energy stored in the nuclei of the atoms. This energy is transferred mainly into light and heat: it has been calculated that at the centre of the Sun the **temperature** is around 14,000,000 °C, which means that an astonishingly vast quantity of energy is involved.

The reactions that power the Sun are known as **nuclear fusion** reactions. In these, the nuclei of hydrogen atoms collide and join together, or fuse. This forms helium atoms and large amounts of energy. Scientists have spent years searching for ways of using this reaction to produce usable energy here on Earth (see diagram opposite), but so far they have been unsuccessful.

Nuclear fission

There is another type of nuclear reaction, **nuclear fission**. If a large nucleus that is already slightly unstable (for instance the nucleus of a uranium atom) is hit by a **neutron**, it may split into two smaller, stable nuclei. More neutrons and a huge amount of energy are released in the process. The amount of energy produced by the nuclear fission of a piece of uranium with a volume of 1 cm^3 is the same as we could produce from a heap of **coal** with a volume of 42,875,000 cm^3.

We have managed to harness this reaction more successfully than nuclear fusion. Nuclear fission reactions are used to provide the energy for a number of electricity-generating power stations. Quite a few of us get the energy we use in our homes every day indirectly from nuclear energy.

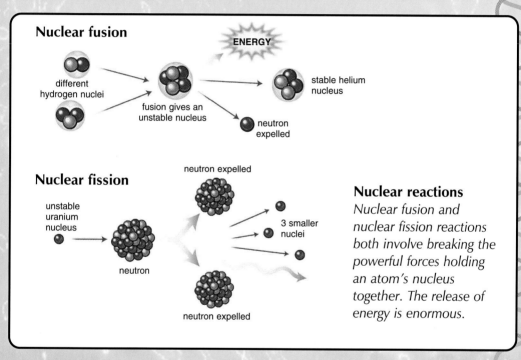

Nuclear fusion

ENERGY

different hydrogen nuclei

fusion gives an unstable nucleus

stable helium nucleus

neutron expelled

Nuclear fission

neutron expelled

unstable uranium nucleus

neutron

3 smaller nuclei

neutron expelled

Nuclear reactions
Nuclear fusion and nuclear fission reactions both involve breaking the powerful forces holding an atom's nucleus together. The release of energy is enormous.

There is another use of the energy produced during nuclear reactions, and this is in the production of atomic bombs and other nuclear weapons of mass destruction. This does not affect us directly in our everyday lives, but the threat of nuclear war in the world is a shadow over us all the time.

As you can see, **potential energy** comes in many shapes and forms and is often invisible and unnoticed. In spite of this, potential energy is as important for the maintenance of everyday life as any of the more obvious and spectacular forms of **kinetic energy** we looked at earlier.

Energy transfers

Go for a walk on a wintry day and your fingers, toes, nose and ears will soon feel chilly. Lie on a sunny beach in the summer and the opposite will happen – the warmth from the Sun will warm you. Turn on a light switch and the room is illuminated. Eat a meal and then play sport and you have the **energy** to keep going for a long time. These things all involve energy transfers. A striking thing about energy is the way transferring it enables us to do something useful.

Faraday and Henry

In 1831 British scientist Michael Faraday developed the first **dynamo** and managed to produce electricity! Joseph Henry was doing similar work in the USA. Faraday published his results first, and is remembered as the discoverer of the dynamo. Faraday was an 'ideas man' – after discovering how to generate electricity he lost interest. Henry, in contrast, was a practical man who went on to develop ways of generating electricity on a large enough scale to be really useful.

Driving with energy

Let's look again at the cars that play such an important role in our lives. We fill them with petrol, a source of **chemical potential energy** when mixed with air. When we turn on the engine the petrol is burned in air to release its chemical potential energy. This is transferred into two types of useful energy – movement energy (accelerating the car) and electrical energy (charging the battery, operating the lights etc) – and two types of wasted energy, heat energy and sound energy. The heat energy is not always wasted. In cold weather we use it to warm up the inside of the car.

Making electricity

Turn on the light. What is happening in terms of energy? Electrical energy flows through the wires and into the filament of the light bulb. As the current flows, the filament becomes hot and glows as electrical energy is transferred to heat energy and light energy. We can see the light energy, and if we hold our hands near the light bulb we can feel the heat energy.

Energy heroes
Michael Faraday (1791–1867) (left) and Joseph Henry (1797–1878) (right) discovered how to make electricity work for us.

We have seen that energy is never lost or destroyed. What happens to the heat and light energy once they leave the light bulb? They spread out though the Universe to become part of the low-grade energy found everywhere in space. In almost every energy transfer some energy is wasted – transferred to a form of energy that is not useful to us, and spreads out until it cannot be useful again.

But where does the electrical energy to light the bulb come from? Generating electricity to fulfil all our needs is a major task, and every **developed country** has massive power stations to do just that. This is another example of the way we use energy transfers. Electricity can be produced when a magnet rotates in a coil of wire. In most power stations we burn **fossil fuels – coal**, natural gas or oil – that are all rich sources of chemical potential energy. As the fuels are burned, heat energy is transferred to water, producing steam. High-power jets of steam drive **turbines** round – more movement energy is in use as the turning of the turbines makes huge magnets turn within massive wire coils. This movement energy is then transferred into electrical energy to supply our homes, hospitals, industries – everywhere where there is a need for electrical energy.

Food for thought

Think about the food you have eaten today, both what you have eaten and how much of it you have had. Now think about all the food you've eaten during the last year. Recent statistics show that the average American teenager consumes around 70 kilograms of sugar and 100 kilograms of meat each year. The food we take in, and the way we use it, make a fascinating story of everyday energy transfer.

An energy chain

All the energy we use in our bodies originally came from the Sun. Plants use energy from the Sun to make food and to grow, transferring the light energy into chemical potential energy in the molecules that make up their cells. People and animals then eat the plants, and also eat animals which have eaten plants, so the chemical potential energy we take into our bodies all comes indirectly from the Sun. Around 10^{19} **kilojoules** of solar energy is used each year by plants to make sugars – an enormous amount of chemical potential energy!

Food factories
Plants transfer light energy from the Sun into chemical potential energy. When we eat the plants we use this energy in our bodies.

Mother power
A baby's whole body has been formed as a result of energy transfers in its mother's body.

What happens to our food?

Think about the last meal you ate – whatever it was it almost certainly was not pure glucose! The food we eat contains high levels of chemical potential energy, but often it is not in a form we can use straight away. The large molecules of carbohydrates, proteins and fats in food need to be broken down in the process of digestion to produce much smaller molecules, such as glucose. The glucose then reacts with oxygen in your body cells to produce more easy-to-use chemical potential energy, plus carbon dioxide and water as waste products and some heat energy. This process is called cellular respiration.

The chemical potential energy produced in cellular respiration is used for all sorts of things. It is used to create new you! Inside your body you are always forming new cells used to make you grow bigger, to replace cells that have worn out and to repair damage when you hurt yourself. This chemical potential energy is also used for moving – energy is transferred in your muscles to move you about. Yet more of the chemical potential energy of your food is transferred to heat energy, to keep your body warm even when your surroundings are cold.

As well as all the food you use in producing energy, there is much that you cannot digest and that passes straight through your gut. If you think about the tonnes of food you have taken in during your lifetime, compared to the amount you now weigh, you will realize that the percentage of chemical potential energy in your food that is actually transferred into new you is very small indeed!

Avoiding energy transfers

In many countries, we have to heat our homes to keep ourselves warm when the weather is cold; some of the heat we create to do this is lost. Because it is colder outside the house than inside, heat energy is transferred to the cooler area and wasted. How can we stop this happening?

Preventing heat loss

Half of the energy used in Western Europe goes to heat and light the buildings we live and work in – our homes, schools, hospitals, shops, offices and factories. That is an enormous amount of energy – particularly when, as the picture below shows so clearly, much of it is wasted. Heat energy that escapes by **convection**, **conduction** and radiation from our buildings is lost to us – it spreads out to become part of the low-grade useless energy of the Universe.

Modern houses are usually designed to reduce the transfer of heat energy from the inside to the outside world. Older houses are less energy-efficient, and can feel cold and draughty.

Hot house
This photo has been taken using an infrared camera. The white areas are where the most heat is escaping – mainly through the windows.

Reducing energy transfers from buildings

- Choose materials, such as concrete breeze-blocks, that are poor conductors of heat.
- Have a cavity between walls, filled with insulating material like plastic foam or beads.
- Double, even triple glazing – two or three layers of glass with layers of air (a poor conductor of heat) between them – cuts heat loss considerably.
- Smaller windows mean reduced heat energy loss.
- Insulating material in the roof space dramatically reduces energy loss through the roof.

In some areas the task is to cool the inside **temperature** down. Air-conditioning systems use electrical energy to move heat energy from the air inside a house or car to the outside. Air-conditioning systems work in the same way as the fridge in your kitchen. The features that help reduce heat loss from a warm house in cold weather help prevent heat getting into a cool house when it is hot outside.

Insulating ourselves

Our bodies, just like our homes, transfer heat energy to the world around them. We need to cover those areas that lose heat most with insulating layers of materials that conduct heat poorly. Up to a third of our body heat loss occurs through our heads, so in cold weather it is really important to cover the head to reduce heat energy transfers. Several layers of clothing will trap layers of insulating air and reduce our heat loss, while gloves and warm socks help reduce heat loss from our extremities. Wearing the right clothes reduces the amount of heat energy we lose on a cold day, and makes all the difference between enjoying the snow and feeling cold and miserable.

For most of us, reducing heat energy transfers is simply a case of making life more comfortable, but for elderly people, and people walking and climbing in exposed areas, reducing heat loss can mean the difference between life and death from the cold.

Energy resources

We have looked at a host of examples of the role **energy** plays in our everyday lives. Now, where does all that energy come from? There are a number of different answers, but one of the major sources of energy we use here on Earth is – fossilized sunlight! To find out just how we manage to do that, read on.

Trees for energy

There is nothing like sitting around a log fire on a cold winter's evening. Burning wood is another way in which we use energy from the Sun. The **chemical potential energy** in the wood came from the sunlight energy transferred to the tree as it **photosynthesized**. When we burn the wood in air, the process of combustion releases that chemical potential energy and transfers it to heat and light energy in the flames.

While it is easy to see how energy from the Sun is transferred to our food and into our wood, it may come as rather more of a surprise to realize that the petrol we pour into our cars also contains chemical potential energy transferred from the Sun. What is more, much of the electricity we use has also ultimately come from the Sun. How? To answer that question we need to travel back millions of years through the history of the Earth, to the formation of **fossil fuels.**

Sunny energy
Whether we eat plants or plant-eating animals, the energy we eat has been transferred from the light energy of the Sun.

Time traveller
Coal is a fossil fuel. These fossilized leaves once photosynthesized under a prehistoric Sun.

Ancient energy

In prehistoric times the Earth was covered in lush vegetation. Many of the plants were giant, tree-sized versions of the brackens and ferns we see today. Prehistoric plants relied on the Sun for food just as modern plants do, and they used the food they made to build up new plant material containing chemical potential energy.

When these massive plants died, layer upon layer of them built up. These were covered with sediments of sand and mud, which over millions of years turned to rock. Often the dead plants rotted away, but sometimes they were simply crushed and covered. When that happened, over time, the plants became fossils, which we discovered millions of years later and called **coal**.

Coal is a shiny black substance that contains the concentrated chemical potential energy transferred from the Sun into those prehistoric plants. It has been mined from the Earth and used as a source of heat and light energy for hundreds of years. Nowadays its main use is as a fuel for the generation of electricity in power stations. The heat energy produced when it is burned in air is transferred to movement energy in the **turbines** and then into electrical energy for us to use.

More fossil fuels

For many years **coal** was probably the best-known **fossil fuel**, but now the one most people think of first is oil. Crude oil is refined to provide us not only with the fuels for our cars, lorries and aircraft but also with many of the chemicals we use to make plastics and other everyday materials, and the fuel for many of our power stations.

Making oil

Crude oil is a thick, smelly black or brown sludge that is extracted from the ground in the Middle East, America, Russia, China and to a small extent in Britain, where it is mainly found under the sea. It is one of the most valuable resources we have, because of the tremendous amount of **chemical potential energy** it contains. Once again this originally came from the Sun.

Millions of years ago in the early seas there were tremendous numbers of tiny plant-like organisms (phytoplankton) floating in the water and making food by capturing the **energy** of the Sun in the process of **photosynthesis**. These organisms were the food supply of huge colonies of similarly tiny animals, known as zooplankton, and they in turn were the food of other small sea creatures such as shrimps. When these tiny animals and plants died they sank down to the bottom of the sea to form a sludgy layer. Over millions of years, layers of sand and mud were deposited on top of the dead animals and plants and formed sedimentary rocks. The action of heat and pressure on the decayed remains of the organisms resulted in the formation of crude oil, usually with a layer of natural gas on top. So, as with coal, the chemical potential energy in crude oil and natural gas came originally from the Sun – our fossil fuels are really fossilized sunlight!

Black gold!
Crude oil is a concentrated source of chemical potential energy. Countries with large oil deposits depend on it for wealth and power.

Energy scores

Different types of energy resource contain different amounts of energy. We value fossil fuels so highly because they are a concentrated energy store – we can use a relatively small amount to produce a lot of useable energy. Fossil fuels are a much more efficient source of energy than plant material grown now, such as wood, as we can see from their relative energy values per gram: wood 20 **kilojoules**, coal 27 kilojoules, oil 42 kilojoules and gas 55 kilojoules. Natural gas is the fuel that contains the most chemical potential energy ready for transferring, closely followed by oil. They are concentrated because huge quantities of animals or plants have been squashed together under great pressure to make them.

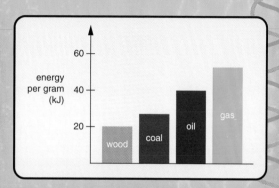

Global energy unit

When we are looking at the world's energy consumption, we do not think about grams of fuel! We talk about '**million tonnes of oil equivalent**' – in other words, the amount of energy in one million tonnes of oil. This unit is used by the energy industry all over the world to make fair comparisons between different fuels. One tonne of oil equivalent is about 40,000,000 kilojoules!

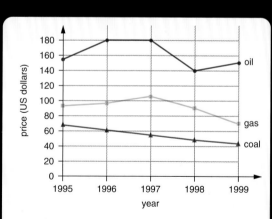

Fuel price graph

This graph shows the changes in price of oil, coal and natural gas in the late 1990s, given in US dollars per tonne of oil equivalent.

Problems with fossil fuels

We have examined how we benefit from different forms of energy. There are, however, some negative factors we must consider if we are to continue to have cheap energy at our fingertips for the rest of our lives.

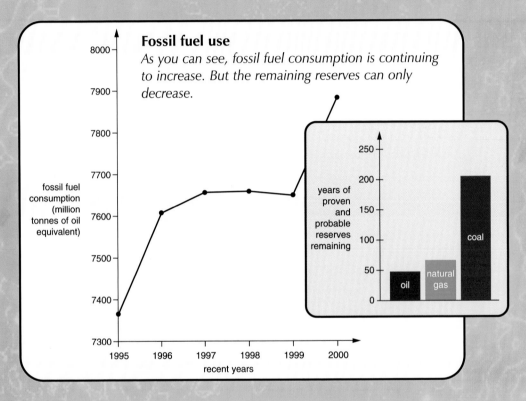

Fossil fuel use
As you can see, fossil fuel consumption is continuing to increase. But the remaining reserves can only decrease.

If you read newspapers or magazines or watch current affairs programmes on TV you will know there are problems with our usage of fossil fuels. One is that fossil fuels are just that – fossils, formed millions of years ago. There is a limited supply of them. In fact, the amount of coal, oil and natural gas left for us to mine and drill is very limited indeed.

A finite resource

People in the developing world use only a fraction of the energy we use in the **developed countries**. For example, North America uses around 1354 million tonnes of oil equivalent of fossil fuels each year, while the whole of Central and South America only account for 325 million tonnes of oil equivalent, and India only 255.5 million tonnes.

We cannot predict exactly when fossil fuels will be used up, because new reserves are found from time to time, and the technology available to extract every last bit of them is improving. But it is clear we must find other ways of generating energy in the near future.

Polluting the planet, destroying our world

When fossil fuels burn, the energy released can work for us. However, not only is some of this energy wasted, chemicals are produced that we do not want and that damage the world. Carbon dioxide – a greenhouse gas – is a product of burning fossil fuels. As the carbon dioxide content of the atmosphere increases, it provides an insulating layer that prevents the Earth losing heat by radiation. Because of our use of fossil fuels, carbon dioxide levels have been climbing for years and Earth's climate seems to be warming up as a result. When we burn 1 tonne of oil equivalent of each of the fossil fuels, we get huge amounts of carbon dioxide – oil produces 3.2 tonnes, gas 2.4 tonnes and coal 4.1 tonnes. So we are creating global warming. This threatens the climate of the world. As the ice caps melt and sea levels rise, whole countries may disappear under the sea, and areas may become uninhabitable hot, dry deserts.

Coal and oil also give off other gases, such as sulphur dioxide and nitrogen oxides. These combine with water in the atmosphere to form **acid rain** and chemical smogs, causing damage to the environment and to our health. Acid rain has killed forests and lakes across Europe and the USA, and damaged many buildings. Pollution from car fumes brings smogs to our cities as well as asthma, bronchitis and other breathing problems. No wonder scientists are seeking alternative ways to provide our energy.

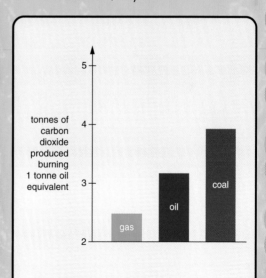

The downside of fossil fuels
High levels of carbon dioxide and the effects of acid rain and other fuel-related pollution threaten our everyday way of life and our health.

Energy in the future

It can seem depressing, looking at the problems of using **fossil fuels**. Still, some very interesting alternatives to fossil fuels are already in use, for generating electricity, for example. More ideas are being developed as **energy** sources of the future.

Energy alternatives

What about now? What are the alternatives to **coal**, oil or gas as fuels in our power stations? Nuclear energy, which we looked at on pages 32 and 33, is one well-used alternative to fossil fuels. It has huge potential, but many problems. Geothermal energy, using the heat from under the Earth's surface, is a very effective energy source in areas where it is available, such as Iceland and some US states. The other alternative energy sources in use are often called renewable energy because, unlike fossil fuels, they can be used repeatedly without running out. When you play computer games or turn on the light you could be using electricity generated using one of these cleaner resources – you would never know the difference, because the resulting electrical energy is exactly the same.

Water power

Water in a river approaching a waterfall has massive **potential energy**, and as it rushes downwards this potential energy is converted into **kinetic energy**. We have harnessed this energy in **hydroelectric power**. Water collects in an upper reservoir, usually behind a dam. It is allowed to fall to a lower level under control, through massive pipes, and its force is used to drive large **turbines** that generate electricity. Hydroelectric power is clean and efficient. It is easy to control the amount of electricity made, and the power stations can be hidden underground or within the dam itself. The main problem is that you need a massive water source, and building dams can have a negative impact on the local environment. All over the world many villages – up to a million people's homes – have disappeared under water for hydroelectric schemes. The water can also provide breeding grounds for malaria mosquitoes and affect agriculture in the surrounding area.

Wind power

People have been
using wind power for
centuries, to grind corn
in windmills. Now we have
wind farms to generate
electricity. Massive wind turbines
are erected in windy areas. As the wind
drives spinning blades, the kinetic energy is used to turn turbines
and generate electricity. Wind power is virtually pollution-free,
although the blades can be noisy and sometimes interfere with radio
signals. Some people object to them because they feel they spoil
beautiful countryside. Offshore wind farms will probably solve this
problem and generate even more electricity – it is usually windy
out at sea! But the high cost of building and maintaining offshore
wind farms is also a factor.

Solar energy

So much energy from the Sun falls on our Earth, and so much of our
energy started in the Sun, it would be fantastic if we could tap this
effectively infinite resource. We can do this in several ways. You may
have a solar-powered calculator. A photovoltaic or solar cell transfers
the light energy from the Sun into electrical energy to help with your
maths! The same thing on a bigger scale can be used for electricity,
or heating a house. Solar energy can also be used to heat up water in
massive boilers, producing steam that is used to drive turbines and
generate electricity.

Conserving energy

Think about the future and how you imagine yourself in 20, 30 or 40 years time. Whatever you hope to be, you will almost certainly want a nice home and a car, and to have plenty of readily available **energy**. One of the biggest problems we face over the next 50 years is how to supply the energy we all want and need without devastating our planet. We are facing a genuine energy crisis, but not everyone is taking it seriously or looking for solutions. It is easy to thoughtlessly continue using energy. Many people are working hard on the problem, though. They are taking two different approaches.

Energy efficiency

One approach to the energy crisis is to increase our energy efficiency. Switch a light on. One traditional light bulb illustrates clearly how much energy we waste, because they are particularly bad at transferring electrical energy into light energy. Only a tiny part of the electrical energy from the mains supply ends up as light energy – most of it becomes wasted heat energy. Modern 'low energy' light bulbs do a much better job, producing a bigger percentage of light and far less heat. Furthermore, they last longer and so save energy in their production as well.

Bright idea
One normal light bulb uses the same amount of energy as four energy-saving light bulbs.

Aluminium efficiency

Aluminium is extracted from its ore using electricity. In the last 50 years:

- the amount of electrical energy needed to produce 1 tonne of aluminium has fallen by over a third
- 54.1% of the electricity used worldwide to produce aluminium now comes from renewable hydroelectric power
- modern cans are thinner, requiring 40% less aluminium
- recycling aluminium has become common. Making aluminium from recycled material takes only 5% of the energy needed to extract the same amount from the ore.

Re-use it or lose it
Recycling is vital to make energy reserves last longer. Some countries recycle up to 80% of household waste.

It is not only light bulbs that can be made more efficient – there are efficiency developments in all sorts of areas. These include house design, to produce houses with minimal heat loss, and car design, to produce cars that use less fuel. In some countries, such as the USA, where petrol remains very cheap, there is relatively little consumer awareness or demand for energy-efficient cars, but in many European countries, including the UK, fuel economy is an important selling point.

Recycling

Another important area is the recycling of materials. We use lots of energy to extract materials such as metals from the Earth, then use them once and throw them away. From cars and computers to food packaging, people are working to make more things that can be recycled. Recycle your aluminium drinks cans! Far less energy is used in recycling aluminium than in extracting it from its original ore.

As we become more aware of the value of recycling, and develop the technology to recycle a wider range of materials, worldwide energy savings will be considerable. If we are more energy-efficient, our fossil-fuel reserves will last longer, giving us more time to develop effective alternative energy resources.

The power of poop!

Nuclear, hydroelectric and wind power are the main alternative sources of energy in use at the moment, but the technology for harnessing other good energy sources is already being developed.

Waste matters

Biogas generators are allowing communities all over the world to produce methane gas, either to supply heat energy or to generate electricity.

Biological fuels are making an impact. In many less developed parts of the world small **biogas generators** are being used to produce energy at family or village level. We all have to eliminate body waste regularly, and plant-eating animals produce vast quantities of dung. Biogas generators are small units containing micro-organisms that break down faeces and food waste and produce methane gas (the same chemical as the natural gas found with crude oil). This gas burns relatively cleanly to provide heat energy for cooking, heating water or electricity generation. This can happen on a larger scale in the **developed** world. People are working to develop the technology to produce biogas generators to be used with the rubbish we produce every day in the preparation of our food.

Biofuels

Gasohol and **biodiesel** are less polluting alternatives to petrol and diesel, and both will be made more widely available. **Ethanol** (the 'alcohol' in alcoholic drinks) produced from sugar-cane was first used as fuel for cars in South America. Now many US states produce 'gasohol', a mixture of alcohol (made from maize) and ordinary petrol, which burns more cleanly than pure petrol and is a partly renewable resource.

Biodiesel is diesel made from plants such as soybean. It can be used in ordinary diesel vehicles and is a completely renewable resource. It just needs plenty of land and good growing conditions. In future, **genetic engineering** may help by allowing scientists to develop high-yield biodiesel crops that grow faster in poor conditions.

Fuel cells - energy for the future

The energy produced in many spacecraft comes from **fuel cells**, devices rather like batteries that make use of the stored potential energy in molecules to make electricity. Fuel cells (or 'hydrogen cells') are one of our most exciting prospects for future energy production. They are compact and clean – the water produced by fuel cells in US space laboratory Skylab was used for washing and drinking.

If fuel cells take over our electrical energy production we could conserve fossil fuels and reduce pollution. Several types of fuel cell are being developed, some suitable for large-scale electricity generation in power stations. Others could be used in cars, for lighting the home or in portable gadgets. Electricity generated through the reaction between hydrogen gas and the oxygen in the air in fuel cells, may be the picture of energy in years to come.

About the future, two things seem certain. Our energy demands will continue to grow – and science and technology will enable us to meet those demands in an ever more environmentally friendly way.

Fuel cells - pros and cons

Pros
- They can use the air around us.
- They are versatile, can generate energy at all levels.
- They are water-based, using the simple reaction between hydrogen and oxygen, producing water.

Cons
- It is difficult to find a readily available supply of hydrogen.

Summary: our energetic Universe

Energy underpins everything. The whole Universe, as well as our life, depends on it. We use energy in many different ways, from the **chemical potential energy** that keeps our cells working to the light energy from the Sun that gives plants food. We make use of energy transfers to provide us with exactly the energy we need in the right place at the right time.

World-friendly driving
Shell run an annual competition for the most fuel-efficient car. This car, made by Andy Green, finished fourth in 2002. It averaged 5191 miles (8352 kilometres) per gallon.

Electrical energy is vitally important for our way of life in **developed countries**. Electricity provides us with heating, lighting and all the different technologies we rely on to make our lives comfortable. But because of the environmental damage caused by burning **fossil fuels** to generate electricity, we need to think carefully about the way we use electrical energy and the ways we produce it.

Today's world energy crisis involves more than just electricity. More and more people all over the world own cars, and cars burn fossil fuels as their supply of chemical potential energy. Scientists are working both on alternative, cleaner energy sources and on ways of making our energy use more efficient.

Energy is involved when we throw a ball into the air, and when water cascades over a waterfall. Light energy illuminates our days and our nights, while sound energy gives us information about the world and allows us to communicate rapidly and easily. Chemical potential energy allows many things to happen exactly when we choose, such as turning on a torch or moving our legs to walk about. Energy means life – enjoy it!

Glossary

acid rain rain with high acid content due to pollution, damaging to the environment

biodiesel form of diesel fuel made from the breakdown of plant oils

biofuels, biological fuels fuels made from the breakdown of biological material

biogas generators generators for making biogas from plant or animal waste decaying in the absence of air

calibrate ensure that a measuring instrument gives accurate readings

calorie unit of heat energy, sufficient to raise 1 gram of water by 1 °C

calorimeter instrument for measuring the energy content of food

calorimetry measuring the energy content of food

cellulose complex carbohydrate found in plant cell walls

chemical bond force holding atoms together in a molecule or crystal

chemical potential energy energy held in a chemical bond that is released during reactions

coal carbon-based fuel made from the fossilized remains of prehistoric plants

conduction movement of heat or electricity through a substance

conductor substance through which heat or electricity can flow

convection transfer of heat through a fluid by currents within the fluid

corrosive slowly damaging by chemical reaction

developed countries wealthy nations that dominate the global economy

dynamo generator that converts mechanical energy into electrical energy

elastic potential energy energy stored in an elastic substance when it is stretched or compressed

electrons subatomic particles with a negative charge

energy capacity to do work

ethanol simple alcohol, C_2H_5OH

flex bend

fluid substance that can flow, i.e. a gas, vapour or liquid

fossil fuel fuel formed over millions of years from the remains of animals or plants

friction force that affects surfaces in contact with each other, slowing down or preventing movement

fuel cell device that produces electricity by oxidizing a fuel

gamma rays type of electromagnetic radiation

genetic engineering directly altering or manipulating the genes of an organism to produce a desired quality

hydroelectric power electrical energy produced from the energy in moving water

insulator material that reduces the flow of heat, sound or electricity, a poor conductor

kilowatt unit of power

kinetic energy energy associated with movement

kJ (kilojoule) unit of energy equal to 1000 joules

mass amount of matter contained in a body

matter something with mass and volume; it takes up space

million tonnes of oil equivalent amount of any fuel that contains the same amount of energy as a million tonnes of oil

negative charge electric charge of the type carried by electrons

neutron subatomic particle with no charge found in the nucleus of an atom

newton unit of force

nuclear fission reaction in which the nucleus of an atom splits into two smaller nuclei, releasing energy

nuclear fusion reaction in which two small, light nuclei fuse together to form a single heavier nucleus releasing energy

nuclear reaction reaction involving the nucleus of an atom

photosynthesis process by which plants make food from carbon dioxide and water using energy from the Sun captured using chlorophyll

positive charge electric charge of a type opposite to the charge carried by electrons

potential difference difference in energy between two parts of an electric circuit

potential energy energy that is stored in a system, e.g. because of its position

power rate of energy transfer, measured in watts

proton heavy positively charged subatomic particle found in the nucleus of an atom

reflect bounce sound, light or heat back from a surface

refract bend of a beam of light as it passes from one material to another of different density, e.g. from air to water

sonic boom extremely loud explosive sound produced when something accelerates past the speed of sound

static electricity electrical charge that builds up on an object as electrons are either rubbed off or deposited on to it

temperature measure of how cold or hot something is

thermometer instrument for measuring temperature

thermostat instrument for controlling temperature

transformer device that changes the voltage in an electrical system

turbine machine for producing power

ultrasound sound where the frequency of the sound waves is higher than can be detected by the human ear

vacuum space containing nothing

voltage electromotive force or potential difference expressed in volts

watt unit of power

work transfer of energy from one system to another

X-ray type of short-wavelength electromagnetic wave that can pass through many materials, used to obtain photographs of the inside of the body, etc.

Finding out more

Books

The Dorling Kindersley Science Encyclopedia (Dorling Kindersley, 1999)

Energy for Life series, by Robert Sneddon (Heinemann Library, 2003)

Fascinating Science Projects: Heat and Energy, Bobby Searle and
 Catherine Ward (Franklin Watts, 2002)

Focus on Science: Heat and Energy, by Nigel Hawkes
 (Franklin Watts, 2003)

Green Files: Future Power, by Steve Parker (Heinemann Library, 2003)

Horrible Science: Killer Energy, by Nick Arnold (Scholastic, 1999)

Websites

www.british-energy.co.uk/education
This is the website of the British nuclear industry. It has a lively
education section.

www.bg-group.com
This website of the British Gas Group has information about the use of
natural gas and environmental issues.

www.nmsi.ac.uk
This gives access to the London Science Museum, where lots of exciting
stuff on energy can be found.

www.state.hi.us/dbedt/ert/electgen.html
This site has some bright diagrams and lots of information about how
electricity is generated.

Other ideas

The Sellafield Nuclear Reprocessing Plant, in Cumbria, is a great location
for a day out. It will give you the chance to consider all sorts of
questions about energy and how we use it.

Index

Titles in the *Everyday Science* series include:

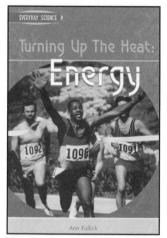

Hardback   0 431 16744 3

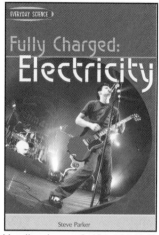

Hardback   0 431 16742 7

Hardback   0 431 16745 1

Hardback   0 431 16743 5

Hardback   0 431 16741 9

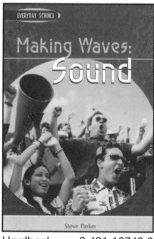

Hardback   0 431 16740 0

Find out about the other titles in this series on our website www.heinemann.co.uk/library

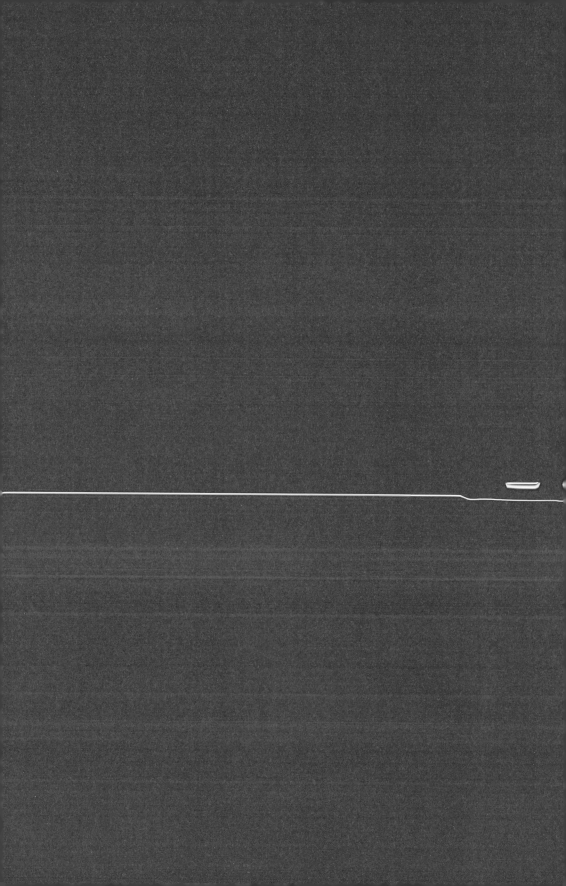